A Self, a Frame, a Look in Through

A Self, a Frame, a Look in Through

Poems by

Ashley Mabbitt

© 2024 Ashley Mabbitt. All rights reserved.
This material may not be reproduced in any form, published,
reprinted, recorded, performed, broadcast,
rewritten, or redistributed without
the explicit permission of Ashley Mabbitt.
All such actions are strictly prohibited by law.

Cover design: Shay Culligan.
Cover image: Leslie Ann Ravel: *Prisms I*, 2013.
Copyright © Leslie Ann Ravel, 2024.
Photograph by Randy Dodson. All rights reserved.

ISBN: 978-1-63980-556-3

Kelsay Books
502 South 1040 East, A-119
American Fork, Utah 84003
Kelsaybooks.com

Dedicated to my late grandparents

Frances & Robert Cox
Margaret Ann & Robert Mabbitt

Acknowledgments

Thank you to the following publications, in which versions of these poems previously appeared:

The Avocet Weekly: "Anna Hummingbird"

The Ekphrastic Review: "Woman working," "On the water"

Plume: "Longing," "Oak leaves as young musicians"

Ravensperch: "Cradling them free"

South Florida Poetry Journal: "Velazquez' lost portraits"

Contents

My ideal self as a small, oval mirror framed in
    gold   13

I.

Alarm clock   17
Husband, wife, and mistress in a room filled with
    antiques   18
Equerry   19
Man and reclining woman who dreams   20
Violetta   21
This   23
The coyote's howl   24
Ink on paper   25
Velazquez's lost portraits   26
Woman working   27
Santiago   28
A few flakes (remain)   29
My ideal self as a hut in the shadow of a great
    mountain beside several vertical lines of Chinese
    calligraphy   30
Figure of a Bijin   31
Final movement   32

II.

My ideal self as a dozen fine point black pens
    stacked inside a clear, plastic drawer in a
    stationery store   35
Black ink   37
Moon jar   38
What is before us today   39
Mountain in Petropolis looks in through a cracked
    open window   40

To my friend Liz's stomach	41
Study of a Mourning Figure	42
Imagining a self-portrait's beginnings	43
Remnant	44
Dream vocabulary	45
Lady of the Evening Faces	46
Cradling them free	47

III.

My ideal self as a sable cookie on a baking sheet just out of the oven	51
Born on the 6th of January	53
First to volunteer	54
The things she told	55
On the water	56
Nothing about you	58
Lost arts of the South Raccoon River	60
The abolitionist farmer's third-eldest son	61
The trouble with Uncle Freddy	62
Dawn prayers	63
Anna Hummingbird	64

IV.

My ideal self in deep time on the eastern shore of Lake Michigan	67
Dishwasher	69
"The Nativity"	70
Call back	71
'55 Mercury	72
Sargent's women in charcoal	73
New England winter	75
Splinter & snap	76

Gooseberry fool (with a splash of brandy)	77
Obedient bodies	78
Longing	79
Elegy (of sorts)	80

V.

My ideal self as a light atop a pole at Newark Airport	83
Earthenware woman	85
Hakata Station	86
The signalman in his high and narrow tower	87
Three Musicians	89
For your new year	90
Before it is turned	91
Our Lady of Fátima	92
Oak leaves as young musicians	93
Hers to mend	94
Eclipse	96
Wolf	97
"Seated Bather with Feet Apart"	98
Momentary doubt	99
My ideal self as a Christmas cactus in bloom	100

My ideal self as a small, oval mirror framed in gold

Whatever passes before me, it belongs,
and I hold it within my frame, lightly,
until it should pass away again.
I have no corners, no narrowed places
where shadows might hide.
I do not break and then continue,
I just continue. As the sky is cornerless
and holds its place while sun, moon, clouds, smog, and stars
lay their tracks and route trains across
its fields: my visitors are fewer in variety
than the sky's, but even for me,
in early spring, great flocks of migrating birds cross my surface.

I.

Alarm clock

Nestled deep in the center of a carton whose outward-facing,
black-marker-scrawled label makes no mention of its presence

inside that particular container—it cries out:

a trembling, high-pitched shriek nearly 12 hours after
its delivery from storage, as if sensing that freedom

were now possible, if only it made itself known.

Husband, wife, and mistress in a room filled with antiques

If the three of you were here—a room of gleaming oak beams,
antique tapestries hanging from cream-colored walls,
scenes of saints and sheep,

and if you were here
as pendulum clocks,
at the top of each hour,

your proclamations,
your spoken voices,
would all sound different notes:

one low and deep,
as if connected to the Earth's core,

another's song soft like clouds
scattering to reveal
pinpricks of starlight,

and a third clear and bright as a single round orange—

but you would all speak
at the same moment,
all at once,

and then return
to tick-tocking steadily
through the next 59 minutes,

surrounded by cherubs blowing into golden trumpets,
and long, slanted rectangles of sunlight creeping

across the floor, bending themselves in half
where oak and plaster meet,

then quarter inch by quarter inch, unbending again,
lighting the cold, flat eyes of woven angels.

Equerry

The brush of a clean, wet pair
of pantyhose, falling from a wooden
drying rack onto the top of your foot

as you stand before your bathroom mirror,
taking care to coat your smallest lashes,

the ones in the corners of each eye,
with your wand of mascara—you sense them landing

but wait to look full on at what is there.
Whereas the brush of a young princess' fingertips

releasing a thimble of fluff from the tunicked shoulder
of a married man (decades older) was small,
but cupped in the palms of so many watchers' eyes.

Man and reclining woman who dreams

"Homme (Apollo)" and "Femme couchée qui rêve"
—Alberto Giacometti

He is firm—
not letting us in.
His lines bending outward
from his center—
this is the extent to which
his vulnerabilities can be glimpsed.

She considers
this resolute reluctance
in her mate,
as she sips from a straw
tipping toward her red lips,
and decides it is shameful really,

like waking up
and consciously banishing
all trace memories
of the most uncanny images
left lingering
from one's dreams.

Violetta

Is she right about love?
Is she right to fling her
red high heels into the center
of the stage and skip barefoot
to the country with Alfredo?

If it were happening now,
a friend might ask her,
Does he have a job?
Where does he live?
What are his friends like,
and his parents?

Of course she herself had a job, that is
until she left Paris, and began
dipping into her savings
to support her great new love.

A question I might ask:
have you calculated the penalties for making
early withdrawals from your 401K?

And of course that isn't the point.
Anyway, her body was fading
in spite of all of this, whether she
loved one man deeply, or plenty
of men a little. Whether she walked
barefoot, or in red heels.

A friend might ask, *does he take you*
to doctor's appointments?
Does he let the dishes pile up
because you are not well enough
to take care of them?

What was it like: waking up
in the morning, before Alfredo stirred, lying
near enough to feel the warmth of his back
and legs, her eyes closed, one arm over a quilt,

feeling sunlight grow steadier through a nearby window,
and a branch, not yet full of leaves,
tapping against the glass every so often,
waiting for the tapping sound to come again?

This

is not it.
You are not it.
I knew before
but now, now
here you are,
your clothes
and mine
somewhere
on the floor, and
my bedside lamp
switched on
so it's hard
to fantasize, to be
here but not exactly
here, like this.
Ouch.
Did I
say that aloud?
Apparently not.

The coyote's howl

An echo is proof of some(one's) reluctance to let go:
canyon walls quarter-inching the long minute hand
back far enough to revisit the coyote's howl or woodpecker's tap.
An echo is evidence of what we cannot easily let go,
and not just beauty, but also the phone call hastily made
to give advice, unwelcome as ever, met with an auto-pilot retort.
An echo tells us there is something someone hesitates to let go:
canyon walls and adult siblings; spacious birdsong and arguments
    never won.

Ink on paper

Reisai Hanshan, 15th century, Dai-tokyu Memorial Library

In the notch underneath
a beachside cliff,

sheltered, although not from the wind
blowing against her back,
lifting the sleeves of her robe,
and the strands of her black hair,

only the twigs jutting out
from the cliff's sides
witness her full and toothy grin
as she clutches in both hands
the dark object, the kindling,
with which she has just sparked
and released onto the fast-moving winds

the glowing ember of a surprise attack,
a violent spell
of overdue revenge.

It will sail out over the bay,
diminishing to a barely visible pink dot,
before boomeranging back toward land,
gaining strength as it speeds after
its ultimate target, not so safely hidden
in a narrow, crooked, pitch-dark street.

Velazquez's lost portraits

There must have been a woman among them,
alone, but with earthenware jugs
reflecting squares of pure white light,
and maybe an orange
on a rough wooden table,
one green leaf still attached.
The fabric of her sleeves, her apron and
the cloth draped over her hair:
deeply creased (peaks and valleys),
and her eyes set gently but firmly
on some spot beyond the painter's left shoulder,
some fragrance coming from somewhere, maybe
through an opened window, which reminds her
of a time, an easier time, that she can now only just
feel all the way to its edges.

Woman working

Seated Woman Scraping a Parsnip
—Nicolaes Maes

Her eyes focus downward
on the parsnip
as she peels

A faint smile

She loves to work by sunlight
from the window
beside her

Early afternoon
late fall or winter

Morning frost
threaded through the grass
has gone

Somewhere else in the room
just returned from the cold air
must be a quiet man

Red cheeks
hair smelling of wood smoke

Bending at the knee
he opens his palms
to the crackling fire

Santiago

Out for a walk after breakfast in our hotel,
we stop slicing open and covering up the same sore over and over
and say something about the trees, and flowers,
but mainly those amazingly unfamiliar trees,
each leaf the size of a mattress
bending backward farther and farther, leaning down and down,
edges frayed and browning crisp,
eventually to be replaced with a bright green leaf
already forming at the tree's heart.

A few flakes (remain)

Like an imported relish, mustard, jelly
brought home long ago, and long since

crusted over on the inside
(a few flakes of dried yellow muck

ground into the horizontal grooves of the glass bottle's top),

I feel as though I had already disposed of that
bundle of fears, as if in preparation for a journey,

setting my kitchen's refrigerator to rights,
and deciding the bottle was no longer of any use to me.

But this morning when I swung open the door
in pursuit of a splash of cold milk,

there it was in the topmost, narrowest shelf
inside the door, not making a sound but

unmistakably present, the fridge motor humming,
as I felt cold air graze the skin of my right hand

and the old thought taking form that I will never find love again.

My ideal self as a hut in the shadow of a great mountain beside several vertical lines of Chinese calligraphy

On the water beyond
the rocky shore
is the one-stroke shape
of a boat

and the two-dot representation
of a man,
sitting in its middle.
We need not call out

to one another.
I will stay listening
to the rippling, dripping sounds
of water falling

from his oars,
as the man considers
whether to stay afloat,
or be welcomed ashore.

Figure of a Bijin

Unknown artist, Hizen, Japan, c. 1680

Listening to the punchline of a joke at the culmination
of a refined gentleman's complex story with multiple characters

was my first interpretation of the expression on her shiny porcelain
  face,
of her half-moon eyebrows and slightly wry, sideways, red-lipped
  smile,

but it could just as easily be upon entering a dining area to discover
an arrangement of flowers, artfully composed to acknowledge her
  birthday,

or a precocious young girl running past down the street,
calling back to her father to please try and keep up,

or the sudden pattering upon leaves of a steady summer rain, or
  sliding shut
the screen enclosing her own bedroom, wooden frames gently
  colliding,

and turning herself around to find the reflection of a bright moon
  stretching
across the matted floor to where her left toes peek out

from beneath multiple layers of kimono.

Final movement

The final movement, which
I must wait for, must stand
next to the radio
and refrain

from latching onto a new,
incomplete task
in order to hear,

will reveal something
about the beginning,
the first movement,
that I have no way
of seeing otherwise,

like the pink and red juice
and flat, black seeds
inside a watermelon,

which are impossible to imagine
if you only ever saw
its smooth, odorless, green and white shell.

II.

My ideal self as a dozen fine point black pens stacked inside a clear, plastic drawer in a stationery store

When the world goes dim and gently beeps
(occasional sounding of the store's alarm system),

our shiny shells reflect the flourishing that awaits us:
not the individual shapes, curves, dots, or swerves,

but our first landings, the first glides and rolls:
top of the sheet, working downward—dashing back

up, catching a nub, scratching a quick squiggle
(sometimes so scratchy to tear a hole).

What is it we want?
To shape anything our bodies are drawn to.

Black ink

It is not that she faces it exactly,
her chronic condition—

not as powerful as the disease
she vanquished once was,

but powerful enough
to be obeyed, to be coddled, or else
she risks an attack that could defeat her.

It is not that she faces it exactly,
having once even said, "I know
one of these days, it's going to kill me."

She does fear it.

But fears it appropriately.

Enough to make sure her laces
are tied neat and tight,
that her bowls are all stacked and nestled,

that her grown children's kindergarten artwork
is stored and labeled,

and that her entire rock collection
is archived—

a tiny, white rectangle, as you might find
in a natural history museum,
beside each one—the name of the place
where she found it written clearly in black ink.

Moon jar

About 1700, Korea, porcelain

Not the space under its lid,
within the confines of its gently curved sides,

Not the sharp corners of the plexiglass square box
preventing the tip of a finger brushing its milky glaze

Not the march of black letters typed in rows—
its dates, origin, reason for having been bequeathed.

:

Its place is the first summer evening I forget
that trees are not always brimming with green leaves,

each reflecting an upturned palm of steady moonlight.

What is before us today

is like a sailboat with three thin white masts and no sails raised

The captain fears what is to come

My friend has been in the hospital now for several weeks

When or if she will be healed is a mystery

There is no way to know for sure the height of the waves that will engulf her

No knowing how far she will be dragged from her course

The storm might even blow south and forget about her altogether

It might simply leave my chest wrenched up tight in fear of what she stands to lose

She said a few words to me, hard to understand, about places she still wants to go

She reached her left arm up over her head (the right arm rendered useless)

It was as if she saw something beyond the water's surface that she wanted to swim up and put her fingertips around

if only her legs had the power to bring her whole body up into brightness

Mountain in Petropolis looks in through a cracked open window

On the morning her secret injury overcame her, following three days
of insisting to her family she only had a stomach bug, the mountain
   was no longer

hidden under wool blankets of raincloud, and could look out, over
the jumbled villages clinging to hillsides surrounding it. Now it had a
   clear view

from its peak all the way to the cracked-open window of a room
   where, for the first time
in years, a young mother did not rise from bed and stand gazing in its
   direction.

To my friend Liz's stomach

Though it is strange for me to address you directly, I must speak
now, before your entire being is banished from the land you call
    home—
directly south of Liz's heart and lungs, north of her hips, knees, feet.
Though it feels strange for me to address you directly, I must speak
as one who occasionally fed you a dinner, refilled your glass of wine,
and acknowledge the disrobed genetic mutation that makes you an
    intolerable guest.
Though it is strange for me to address you like this, almost intimately,
I speak
now, before your entire presence is purged from the land you call
    home.

Study of a Mourning Figure

Michelangelo

I did not realize at first she was in mourning, only
that her face was partly concealed

by a shadow from the cloth draped over her head
and falling gradually forward, and by her hand,

covering her cheek, palm turned toward her, as if
she pressed her lips to the inside of her right wrist,

and then paused, to console herself, finding
tenderness there—flakes of snow, softer than air,

some (a few) settling into the gently curved shelf of her eyelashes.

Imagining a self-portrait's beginnings

The matte pink peony
she placed in her hair,
sticking stem into
the tight hug of her braids,
is the same flower
her pet spider monkey
picked and brought to her
bedside that morning,
where she lay on her back,
sensing, beneath her blanket,
the presence and absence
of her amputated right foot;
slow twirl and hum
of a ceiling fan's blades.

Remnant

Start it: the bed had no headboard,
and there was no nightstand next to it,
no solid wooden object, or

broken remnant even, floating
on that ocean's surface. Afford
my body—treading water, rescue boat

sinking slowly just beside me—
lend me some shelter, some cove
away from this threatening sea:

Hands rising up and under my clothes,
tugging my hip to turn, face it (him)—oh please,
let my fingers' grip on the mattress seam keep hold.

Dream vocabulary

She never turned upside-down in her dreams,
and she never turned to the ones

who stood beside her
or reached out her arms
to embrace them.

She dealt in lost rings of keys, disorganized
luggage (packed in extreme haste),

and muteness. Muteness like an overcast
sky so uniform, a shift seemed impossible.

She was hardly even aware she owned an entire body,
let alone a right arm, and a left, fingers, ear lobes—

sounds coming to meet her without ever
having paused to define their contours.

Lady of the Evening Faces

To be pleasant, gentle, calm and self-possessed:
this is the basis of good taste and charm in a woman.
                    —The Tale of Genji

Is it a dropping away, an untying
of a white satin sash

that only after dusk does she realize
is still loosely knotted, ineffectively,

as a split and splintered wooden beam
made soft by persistent rains?

Is it only now she gains access, regains access,
to what is stored inside the lacquer gold leaf box?

There she finds her inkstone. Brushes.
There she also keeps incense, its tendril of gray smoke

combing letters in the misty air; gently drumming beat of a sea

beyond the pines enclosing her veranda.

Cradling them free

>"An Old Woman Cooking Eggs"
>—Diego Valazquez

The boy waits, ladle in hand,
his gaze fastened to two eggs
poaching in the old woman's red
clay bowl, but she isn't doling out
anything, her gaze roaming past what can easily
be seen, even as the fingers of her right hand
elegantly grip her wooden spoon, angled
toward the eggs, offering the possibility
of cradling them free.
                        Her spoon angled
the same way the sonogram technician
held her all-seeing wand yesterday, gliding it
through and through the clear gel she'd squeezed
over my right breast, running the wand's eyeball
up from my ribs, in from my armpit, down
from my collarbone, all the while looking
without speaking at the black and white
layers of sediment that were part of me,
but a mathematical equation I had no
hope to solve. With what would she fill
my ladle and send me home?

III.

My ideal self as a sable cookie on a baking sheet just out of the oven

I not only basked in the heat,
its intensity formed and shaped me.

There were many of us who did this,
exposing our whole selves, at first soft and damp,

and then rising to our feet, lifting our chests
to the noonday sun; we felt our fate

meeting us where we stood. And now, at rest,
we await the loosening from the parchment, the levitating mid-air.

Born on the 6th of January

As the season entered its longest period of darkness,
her firstborn-to-be gathered more of the strength

he would need to be born, to be heard and seen,
not merely felt, by his mother. Before Christmas, or

after the start of the new year? The doctor, who lived
close by (the only one in their town) had not made

any prediction based on whatever he could hear
through the listening device he pressed against one ear,

and leaned gently to her gradually rising and falling belly.
On cold but bright mornings, sunlight sometimes lay over

top her soapy hands as they submerged and then re-emerged
from the fresh water she'd drawn to wash the breakfast dishes,

one or two bubbles big and round enough to swirl
bright colors before breaking apart. Was this sunlight actually

powerful, enduring enough that it could be felt deep inside her,
not just on her skin and nails? How else would her child grow

strong enough to take shape, how else would he want to become
so much that he dreamt of a space beyond darkness, close and calm?

First to volunteer

The night before, perhaps Ruby's father, Mr. Bridges, leaned one shoulder
against the doorway into the kitchen, arms crossed over his chest,

and watched as his wife stood in a pool of yellow lamplight,
pressing the last hint of a crease from the curved collar

of a child's brand-new white cotton blouse.

Did he say anything? Ask where it came from?
In nightfall's lull, their argument

from earlier in the day poked out from behind drawn curtains,

but he let it go, knowing tomorrow was already loaded onto a long freight train,

and in the morning, its contents would at last be pried open,
as his daughter stepped up to the school's front door

in her shiny patent-leather Mary Janes, each with a bow at its tip.

But after the first week, a month, after one season, and another,
and still not one other student volunteering to take a desk in the same classroom,

the teacher pretending she taught not to one, single child but to rows of children
with eager hands raised,

after the daily escort of Federal Marshalls,
weekly appointments with a child psychiatrist,

and his wife, each night, ironing every donated blouse, skirt,

and lace-trimmed sock they received,
he packed his case, boarded a train, and never came home again.

The things she told

or didn't tell her daughter fell into three categories:
things she must do,
things she must not do,
and the things she wished she could tell her daughter how to do but
    could not.

The reasons why she could not were obscure to her.

When her daughter, long-since grown,
came for a visit once a year,
her mother could almost see

the shapes of phrases that would be like
spreading a flannel picnic blanket over a bed of grass
so that they could sit or lie down,
feeling sunlight warm their faces and toes.

But she could not, or would not, draw the shapes she imagined.

These visits were always during winter
and at the end of an evening,
after closing up the restaurant she had opened
to help her son, unemployed and solemn,

she would turn out the lights
and lock the door behind them,
her daughter handing over the keys
and looking at her mother, expecting nothing,

waiting for nothing beyond a silent walk,
side-by-side, to the glass bus shelter
where they would stand waiting to board and go home,

waiting and watching their white exhales rise
and disperse in the cold night air.

On the water

"Harbor of Dieppe"
—J.M.W. Turner

A question
shouted over
urns, baskets,
bundles of
cloth tied
tightly,
a cage without
birds, and more
baskets floating
on the water;
as she waits
for her mother
to answer
this question,
which she does
not know
is lost
to the squabbling
pigeons and
people trading
fish nets
and gossip,
her mother
notices her
daughter is,
this morning
in the sun,
a woman
with fine
cheeks and
long fingers—

an expression
on her face—
serious beyond
her years.

Nothing about you

not even your physical appearance:
your four exact corners,
uneven creases,
or your pale greenness,
paling to grimy grayish-green
the longer you circulated,
was unique.

Did you never grow tired
of greasing one palm, then the next,
never developing any deeper
attachment to anyone
who received you
gratefully?
Who held you and kept you safe?

Maybe this is exactly
what you were attempting to do,
to be at rest, to reflect
on your relentless journey,
when you hid yourself, folded neatly
into a deep pocket of my grandma's
warm winter coat,
tucked so efficiently away

that long months later,
when once again
she made her first steps
across the icy parking lot
of a Michigan winter,
you revealed yourself at last,
refraining from hunching up
as far away as you could get
from her fingertips' long reach,

and as she felt your form in her hand,
bringing you out
into the diminishing sunlight
of late afternoon,

she stopped and stared
down at you with an expression
of disbelief,
amazement,
genuine confusion, as to
how she had managed
to keep herself,
her husband, and all three
of her children afloat
last winter, without
a single favor from you,
a perfectly useable
five-dollar bill.

Lost arts of the South Raccoon River

Great Uncle Vernus was a man who knew
his land, the river flowing through it to the nearby dam,

and he knew about ice. How to prepare ice to bring to market,
how to earn a living from it. And he also knew

that around Thanksgiving the surface of the river would freeze.
He watched its movements grow still, fallen snow

dimpling and divoting the water's frozen face. Vernus waited
for the right moment (most years, it was a late December night),

cold and quiet under the stars, and he would cut the gravelly ice
150 yards or so above the dam, letting the running water below

carry all the broken pieces away. Then it was Granddad and his
boyhood friends' turn to watch, as new ice materialized, smooth

as mirror, and firm under their bodies as they skated large and small
loops, overlapping and intersecting, leaving narrow trails behind,

maybe like the loops of the miller's knot that Vernus taught
    Granddad
to tie. Great Uncle Vernus had traded grinding grain for ice—

freezing whole instead of grinding down, breaking apart
to build again as new.

The abolitionist farmer's third-eldest son

Just as he was finishing a day's work, returned from the farthest
   fields,
horses in the barn, snuffling their twitching snouts into burlap bags
   of feed,

his arms tired, upper back too, the ribbon of sky
over the mountains' peaks (still blue but darkening), would reach
   down,

and sink its fingers into the gaps between granite hills.

It was now he could actually believe that, later on, after dinner
with Father and the rest of the family, and Father's nightly sermon,

when he laid down in his bed, moonlight laying over top his legs and
   torso,
his heart would beat as steadily as the interlocking loops of a steel
   chain,

one always following the next, lined up and resting upon the soft,
   green grass
of the valley's floor, but pulled taught and ready—

to halt in place any fallen, rolling boulder, stopping it from crashing
   straight into

their wooden farmhouse as it silently stood, bearing the sleeping
   family inside it
till rays of morning light shot over the jagged rocks surrounding
   them.

The trouble with Uncle Freddy

It was never that he did not try, that he was not a good son
or younger brother; he was the one to enlist
in the Army Air Corps and fly planes during the war.

And while brother Bob opened his own beauty shop,
met his wife playing piano in the church choir,
and left the farm for good with wife and baby girl,

Freddy stayed: his mother silently listening in on neighbors'
telephone calls, and Dad tipping spoonfuls of cod liver oil
down the throats of his ailing chickens or dogs; evenings

sitting all three together, tuned in to a Western on the radio.
Eventually Freddy did marry, and went into business
producing and selling eggs, but there were never children,

and all those new chickens came down with a terrible flu.
Now what we have are Freddy's letters, sent home during
the war. A scrawled, tilting *Dear Folks,* always to start.

How was the weather there, he wanted to know,
ever hopeful of his homecoming well before planting
new seeds in spring's freshly-turned fields.

Dawn prayers

His allotment of familiar sounds (the bird chirps spread beneath
his spring mornings, clomp of horse hooves growing and fading)

were a different set from his father's, born in a country
his son would never hear or see,

and different from the parcel of sounds
which became familiar to the son in war

(during battle, before and after battle).

Those sounds maintained their power to jolt.
Wet winds against tent canvas through the night,

as he listened for dawn to come (a new day revealed
first to his ear, not his eye).

Hushed words of soldiers kneeling in their own tents nearby.
The deep sound of tree roots steadying themselves before the
    cannon fire.

Anna Hummingbird

You sit in a lilac bush in the garden of a middle-aged widower. It is November and you want to be close to the feeder he keeps filled with sugar water, and even thaws for you—he senses your annoyance when it freezes. From his kitchen window, from the other side of a camera lens, he's come to know you. He's even given you a name. Your feathers, brown on your breast, greenish-yellow on your back, splotched white on your motionless wings, stand out as though you shiver. He sends a photograph to family living far away, you in profile on a cloudy day, clumped snow on branches, straight black needle of a beak. You soothe his mother with the thought that her son is now in possession of a certain sense of happiness.

IV.

My ideal self in deep time on the eastern shore of Lake Michigan

A ship speeds north
up the great lake,
covering its miles,
churning the water's
surface as a lap
swimmer racing
between the ropes
of the horizon
and the grassy dunes'
peaks; motor silent
from shore
but creating wind
enough to disturb
fine white curtains,
sheer enough
to permit shadows
of saw-toothed
green leaves
to settle
on the shiny
wood floor
beneath
my feet.

Dishwasher

As Dad put clean glasses
from the dishwasher away,
he kept a towel over one
shoulder, to dissolve
lingering water pooled
in the upturned bottoms
of coffee mugs.

The towel and the
determined look

on his face
made me think
of burping a baby,

that he might be
attending to a newborn,
after having fed
her a bottle and
before putting her
down to sleep.

"The Nativity"

Circle of Donatello

Everyone else is sleeping (even the cow's eyelids
are heavy and barely lift), but she
is awake and watching steadily, her new
son lying on soft, clean cloth, watching
with palms and all ten fingertips pressed together, knuckles
relaxed, thumbs resting against the middle
of her chest, rising and falling with each new breath.

Call back

It was the sound of her inhale that gave her away;
maybe an attempt to clear a path to *hello,*
and the only sound she made before hanging up.

My father stood a few moments more, receiver to ear,
not knowing what his sister-in-law's inhale
had been unable to say,

but with a feeling in his body of melting—
something solid had melted away.

Even if he had told my mother right then
that her sister had called, taken a breath, and hung up,
he could not have guessed what it was

that had actually happened; a death in her family
he supposed, but not a premature one, not the sort
that would require a detailed description for anyone to believe.

And so he waited, silently, for the inevitable call back,
as the earth beneath him gradually turned muddy,
and his shoes began sinking in.

'55 Mercury

Cold winds blew hardest in the dark
when there were no other cars,

over farm fields in Ohio,
whistling through cracks
around our windows and doors,

sweeping ribbons of snow across the road in our headlights.

I went along as Dad's traveling companion
from Fall's Church, Virginia to Chicago,
kept him company as he sat behind the wheel
of our orange '55 Mercury.

As we headed west across Indiana, the sun rising behind us,
sunlight glinted off the rear-view mirror
until Dad reached up, squinting, to give it a swivel.

These images I have still
of the long drive north,
but none from the funeral itself.

All I can see is the plaid wool cap Dad wore, gray and white,
and I hear the wind whistling me to sleep.

Sargent's women in charcoal

1.

Driving through Western Massachusetts the morning after an ice
    storm,
I'm in actual winter finally, whereas back in the city, even in
    December

when I visited a Sargent exhibit one Friday after dark, I wore no hat
or gloves. Over the shoulders and around the heads of other museum
    visitors,

I spotted but was swept past a portrait of the artist's niece and her
    dearest friend
huddled together, draped in a white cashmere wrap. But even in a
    portrait

of charcoal smudges and curving tendrils of hair fallen loose from
    bobby pins,
each woman on the gallery's four walls was pinned to straight-backed
    silence:

barely breathing and utterly still.

2.

Now, surrounded on all sides by a frozen-blue landscape, the artist
and his niece come to mind.

Maybe there was a morning in the Swiss Alps like this: she unlatches
and leans out her bedroom window, wrapped again in cashmere and
　　looking out

over winter tree branches—their every last knuckle encased in glass.

Sargent himself, perhaps returning from an early walk, happens to
　　glance
upward, and see his niece noticing all of this—

sunlight shining through icy branches, not heating or melting,
not altering, but making visible—pointing a pencil tip

at what is already there.
Maybe she leans a little farther, taking a last look, a pause, then pulls
　　the window shut once more.

New England winter

Dad saved money
one New England winter,
chopping wood and feeding it
into the belly of a stove
that burned alongside our TV set.

He chopped just outside the garage,
with a tree stump the size of cocktail table, but lower,
working without speaking,
without looking up,
raising his axe over his head,
and bringing it down exactly
where he meant to—
shearing the one log into a pair,
both of which hopped up and
landed with a *plink-plink* on the driveway cleared of snow.

Dad stacked his split logs just so
against the back of the house,
their woody fragrance concealed under a black tarp,
until, into the fire,
they snapped to.

Splinter & snap

A box of wooden matches
economy-sized
and plenty more to strike

though the bubbled sides
of the box's rib cage
are wearing thin

I struggle to make a fresh
match spark and flame
to strike a staccato

note of fire
to extend a blazing blonde
twig to a quarter-inch wick

and let my eyes almost close
allowing light in beneath the door
when I open my eyes again

the splintered and snapped
matches fire never brought to life
lie scattered on my table

Gooseberry fool (with a splash of brandy)

I'm a fool to fool around with buying a whole pint
of thumbnail-sized, reddish-green globes, seedy and sour.
The one who picked and crowned these berries in a red cloth net
has also just passed a Saturday morning in July, at work, or at rest.
I'm a fool to fool around with buying a whole pint
of the slightly bizarre fruit my grandfather held in high regard.
Humid and stormy all week long—do gooseberry bushes have
    prickly thorns?
I'm a fool to fool around with bringing home an entire pint
of reddish-green globes a stranger took the pains to pick,
all for a loved one who is no longer here to be indulged.

Obedient bodies

A matching pair of white shakers, orange daisies emblazoned
at precise intervals, circling their hips,
were handed to me straight from Martha's cupboard
without her knowing a thing about it.

I tap each one once per bite of jammy egg,
at home on a Saturday morning, considering momentarily
how near the time of untwisting a silver cap and pouring
white salt or black pepper straight down a shaker throat.

A matching pair of white shakers, orange daisies emblazoned
at precise intervals around their hips,
which I suspect Martha kept filled to the very tops
of their necks without fail—how satisfying

to control the fullness of these obedient bodies;
how unlike the glass bottles of scotch her husband poured out
and out every day of the long years they shared together.
A matching pair, these white shakers, orange daisies circling their hips

at exact intervals, were given to me straight
from Martha's kitchen by my uncle, as he gradually
emptied out the entire contents of his dead parents' house.

Longing

It is when they leave that it happens:

standing at your kitchen sink, rinsing a mug with dried coffee rings
in its bottom—you don't drink coffee but keep instant for guests.

It is silence re-forming behind, in front, and to either side

of you, which you somewhat mitigate by switching on the radio.

It is that, but it is also knowing that this wish not to be alone in your
 own home
will evaporate a week from now,

when returning a phone call will become something
you push away to honor your quiet,

all the while unconvinced
a longing evaporated means

you have learned the lesson
it wants so urgently to teach you.

Elegy (of sorts)

A secret, yes, there was sometimes a secret
energy of sorts (is it too imprecise to call it
a hunger?), somewhere between the bottom
of my ribs and the top of my navel, which made
its presence known at times both expected
and surprising—expected like my last summer,

on vacation, riding along in my brother's car after
a hike over and through a grassy landscape glaciers made,
on our way to a farm stand with ears of corn piled
on a wide, wooden table once painted green, by then faded.
How can a feeling of deep satisfaction be something
to keep to oneself?

I suppose, to me, it was out of a sense of delicacy.
If I found that, for a single moment, my touch was gentle
enough to fondle the warm flame of a candle's light,
I did not even want to raise my voice in a whisper,
and anyway, I could never think of the right words
to explain to anyone else how to be as gentle as that.

V.

My ideal self as a light atop a pole at Newark Airport

I'll let the rain roll down my spine
in slow, crystal beads.

Should my light fail,
it will be healed, and made bright again.

A white truck comes into my beam,
and pauses for a moment

before continuing on
to the far end of the runway.

The sun rose a couple of hours ago,
but I'll continue in this way,

illuminating part of a roof,
a section of gray pavement

painted with yellow and white lines—
the paint fading and wet
in the morning's rain.

Earthenware woman

Female musician playing a flute or pan pipe
   —Western Han dynasty, 206 BC

Who was she
this woman who dropped
her flute

      and her hands and wrists?

She holds her arms up,
sleeve ends draping open

in long Os to reveal
      what is missing.
She looks to where

they used to be.

Hakata Station

Just one more—one more after
this train, she bargains, like
her children, pleading for more sweets.
Let one more go by. Sitting on a platform
bench, beside a bottled-drinks machine,
a narrow, horizontal screen blinking
as a new train pulls alongside; recorded
voice, moderate and sure, offering up
its destinations as its white doors slide open.
Let one more pass by, she resolves, paper ticket,
just one, in her plaid coat pocket—as if
she herself were all she had to claim, all she had
to tuck, smooth, lift, bundle, pack, pinch, and pull.

The Signalman in his high and narrow tower

was perched over an empty stage
of East Yorkshire train tracks, sitting
quietly, as his auditorium filled
with bursts of color and sound, then
dropped into near silence, again

and again, from the start
to the end of his shift.
But this time, there was
a variation.

He suddenly spotted,
down the railway, a man
wearing large headphones,
and holding out a microphone
at the end of a long, metal pole.

A totally unscheduled event.

Waving, the signalman climbed
down to the ground and called out
to the man to come near.

Did he know then
that he was slated to be succeeded
by an automated machine?

Did he know, and then see
the man making a recording
as his last, best chance

to capture his own notes
and rhythms, perhaps someday
to be plunked out slowly
on some stranger's keyboard?

A short while later, the two sat
side by side, inside the gate box,
leaning slightly forward in their seats
as if over a balcony railing,
so as not to miss the song of a single bird

becoming a duet of two, then overtaken by
a local train crashing through, followed
by a faster one, higher-pitched, as it
covered its long distance, gliding past
the estuary on the far side the tracks.

The signalman took his time, explaining
to the man how he'd learned
this language, composed of bells

and semaphores, which
had kept safe untold people
from untold disasters,

rising to his feet as he spoke, readying
himself to play a momentous note,
as if from the percussion section
of an orchestra pit—calling out, up
and down the line, without saying a word.

Three Musicians

Pablo Picasso

None of them has eyes, only six holes where eyes could be.

A guitar player plucks one string with a pointy finger—pluck, echo,
 pluck pluck, echo echo,
Followed by a strum, flaying all five pointy fingers—strummmmm,
 hummmmm
That hum vibrating through the blue geometric shape he shares
For the top half of his face with
The clarinet player.

The clarinet player's mustache wiggles as he pops a string
Of low notes over to the third musician, who doesn't need
To make a single sound,
Taking it all in through his cheese-grater beard.

Big bright notes make the stained-glass trouser legs of the guitar
 player glow orange and gold
as a dog splayed beneath their chair closes her eyes and basks on.

For your new year

May your new year begin
like a striped beach umbrella, opening
with a muted "pop" sound—its broad,

smooth cloth keeping you cool
on the sand underneath,
as it faces the sun's heat

for you. And may
each hour progress
in its own time; may you find

its wisdom settling easily into you, without
worry that something dear is now lost.
May a place to sit appear when your legs feel heavy,

and may sitting down bring to mind
a memory, a vivid image, of waking up
beside someone who adores you,

on the very first morning
you awoke without doubt
that new love had arrived,

and you had been able
to fully
let it all in.

Before it is turned

your new leaf must first
be found. But even once found,
its hidden underside is still
mysterious. Can it be
relied upon
to open you up
to your potential?
Is the lesson to find
a particular new leaf,
with special knowledge
of your deepest desires,
or will any new one do?
Or are you
already in possession
of this gift you have
been waiting to receive?
What about the shiny, dark green
magnolia down the block:
branches lush in late
December? Of course
it is true we are meant
to think of the other
sort of leaf—the page
in a book. But pages
are filled with words,
whereas a tree leaf
still attached to a winter branch,
which you have passed by,
morning and night,
has been waiting
to share what it knows
with you, for you
to pause long enough
to hear
what it has been
whispering
all year long.

Our Lady of Fátima

*Visitors come to Fátima, Portugal every May to October,
where it is believed that Mary once appeared*

The walking itself is how she will find a new direction.

Not in finally reaching the place itself,
the group of women all together,
stopping to wipe their necks and foreheads with bandanas,
knowing they will not have to begin again early the next morning,
trudging along the roadside, their bright, reflective vests
keeping them visible at dusk and in rain.

No, for this quiet woman, walking faster and faster,
keeping her awareness of a blister forming
on the underside of her left foot vague and muted,
as the sounds of the others talking also become vague and muted,

this is when her best moment will occur.

She will feel her tent strings and poles click into place,
canvas flaps unwrinkling and snapping flat and smooth,
and her floor stretching out over a new bed of soft, green grass.

Oak leaves as young musicians

Frosted-glass lit orange.

She cracks open the window—oak leaves,
wind tossing them recklessly, a reminder
of the time to come:
dispersing, scattering, succumbing.

For now, the leaves lean languorously
up against and over top of one another,
front to back, front to back, checking
what the others are doing.

A high school orchestra chatting
as they tune their flutes, their horns,
their violas and violins.

They will do this, with one another,
until a baton's tapping becomes insistent,
sounding from the curved, metal corner
of a conductor's podium.

Hers to mend

Once, the S-shaped pine tree standing between her house
and the high, wooden gate surrounding it, had no brown needles,

but this morning, as she pinned her clean bedding
to the balcony railing, she stopped to look at its reddish-brown
    clumps.

The rainy season had lasted longer than usual, so why
was the tree protesting against the conditions it had been given?

Her intention, as she went in from the balcony and prepared to
    depart
for a new day's work, was to visit the ancient garden nestled behind

her office building—to sit on a bench with her lunch unwrapped on
    her lap,
and consider the pine, its damaged parts, and possible remedies.

But in fact, she sat and ate beside the garden's large pond,
simply gazing across its surface, and up at the branches extending
    over the water—

sunlit ripplings reflected on the undersides of its leaves,
like the inside of an umbrella opened against bright sun.

Then she remembered the sick tree—hers to mend, and yet,
what cure was she to offer?

When she returned home in the evening, she unlatched the gate,
placed her plastic bags of shopping down on the stony path leading to her door,

and looked upon the ailing one.
As she stood, an image formed in her mind, of a cat, curling up on a rug at someone's feet.

She knelt to the ground and crawled beneath the tree's branches, brown needles imprinting on her palms; as she stretched out and laid on her back, resting her head near the trunk,

she looked up toward the sky, not quite beginning to fade into dusk.

Eclipse

I don't think they even knew,
do you?

How closely we watched
their progress,

how we brow-furrowed every
wisp of cloud which

might clump together
and block our sight of

the sun and moon, walking
their two paths like toddlers

through the morning sky
without pausing to wonder

whether the grown-ups
noticed how freely

they balanced
on their two pairs of

feet, not once clutching
anyone's hand.

Wolf

Chives & sour cream or
nutmeg & egg yolks
in my Christmas Eve potatoes—
I can decide this.

My house stands steady
as the sun and planets rise
and set over its roof,
on its horizons.

In this moment, I am not
feeding the wolf who asks
"but for how long will I feel relaxed?"
Or "What did I forget to bring together?"

I am not concerned with the sword
tucked securely in its case,
and I am not undoing its latches
or running my fingertips along a sharp and narrow edge.

"Seated Bather with Feet Apart"

Auguste Rodin

She might still forget.

She might be able to watch
as the surface of her bath dissolves each recurring thought
she has been unable to see around for days.

Under the surface,

she grips her second toes between thumbs and forefingers,
massaging the places on her feet where toes attach.
Knees and thighs pressed together, but lower legs

wide apart, as she leans her torso forward.

If her face and neck were here with us,

they would glisten with droplets of steam so tiny,
they create a single layer of continuous moisture, over her cheeks,
down her neck, even over the round caps where arms and shoulders
    meet,

and move slightly as she rubs her toes,

thinking whether her thoughts will be satisfied
to stay behind in the bathwater
if she stands up now to leave.

Momentary doubt

The balanced rock starts to slip
off its place atop a larger, rounder stone.
What caused it? Clearly no earthquake,
no dump truck kaboomed down the street
in the moment of slip. It was a tiny
rock thought, some imagining too small
and too quiet for the human ear to notice.
A rock can lose faith momentarily as easily
as can any of us. Doubt trims the legs
of the table where we placed our drinks,
and turning back for another sip, only wet and
broken glass, and a damp, red, square napkin
remain. Even the sounds of steady rain through
the night, or windswept branches, have their momentary doubts.

My ideal self as a Christmas cactus in bloom

Her fuchsia petals never flinch from the light's strength,
its warmth lasting for long winter moments—
but she does not cling to the memory of it.

As the morning light makes geometric shapes
on the floor, walls, and parts of the furniture
nearest the windows,

she stands to one edge,
then the very center,
and finally falls outside the sun's borders.

With quiet expectation of a return,
of fresh water, and spring, each time the light
comes back, she simply lets it look at her for as long as it will.

About the Author

Ashley Mabbitt's poems have appeared in *Plume, The Ekphrastic Review, Emerge, Ravensperch, South Florida Poetry Journal,* and *Summerset Review.* Ashley works in academic journal publishing and is currently writing her second poetry collection. She lives in Brooklyn, New York.

More of her work, and details about the poetry circle she leads, can be found online at:
www.ashleymabbitt.com

www.ingramcontent.com/pod-product-compliance
Lightning Source LLC
Chambersburg PA
CBHW030053170426
43197CB00010B/1502